I0157474

BETTER THAN CHEESE

Cam A. Vuksinich

Illustrations by L. M. Hargrave

Amazing Mouse Books

Better Than Cheese

Copyright © 2014 by Cam Vuksinich

All rights reserved.

No part of this book may be reproduced, scanned, or distributed in any printed or electronic form without permission. Please do not participate in or encourage piracy of copyrighted material in violation of the author's rights. Purchase only authorized editions.

Publisher: Amazing Mouse Books

ISBN: 978-0-9905245-0-2

Library of Congress Control Number: 2014911127

Illustrations: L. M. Hargrave
    lindymhargrave.com

Book and Cover Design: Gary D. Hall,
    GreystrokeCreative.com

Editorial Services: Angela Sims

Printed in the United States of America

Copies of this book may be ordered from:

www.Amazon.com
www.AmazingMouseBooks.com

This book is dedicated to everyone, young and old, who wakes up everyday and chooses to be kind.

BETTER THAN CHEESE

My name is A.M. That's all that there is.
It's like being a bubble with no pop and no fizz.
My Mom and Dad tried really hard you see,
to give me a name that's special like me.

I know that I'm tiny, that's not a surprise.
My dreams sure are big, but I'm pocket-size.
I'd sit by my window and watch the kids play.
I knew I'd be with them and imagined that day.

I watched and believed and learned how to listen.
Being seen and heard makes children's eyes glisten.
The day finally came for me to learn more;
I left for a place where children could soar.

It started with "s" and ended with "ool",
where big kids go that are really quite cool.
I packed my blue bag with pencils and books;
I hoped that my name wouldn't cause funny looks.

I knew on that day that I would stand out.
I didn't know why but there was no doubt.
A mouse with my name is not what you'd guess,
so here is my story. It starts with a mess........

1

My first day at school was filled with confusion.
I'll admit I was scared, but that's no solution.

I was the only mouse in a school filled with kids.
The first time they saw me they flipped their lids!

They noticed my name and started to guess,
"It's only two letters! We're not impressed."

Finally they realized that simple is best;
they gave me a name with no zip and no zest.

Later at lunch, with a bang and a thump,
a thunderous noise came from one little bump.

I wanted to help and wasted no time,
I cleaned up the mess as if it was mine.

The other kids laughed and pointed at my shirt.
It was just a small stain; not big, just a squirt.

The spot I saw was as big as a house!
My favorite shirt! I was a really sad mouse.

"A new spot today? What happened to you?
The spot's always red: not yellow, not blue!"

The spots would show up with no paint or puddle.
It didn't make sense! I was REALLY befuddled.

I watched all my shirts in the spinning machine.
Circling once. Twice. I lost count at umpteen.

"We ALL have a spot! We know who's to blame.
It's the mouse with initials instead of a name!"

I went to the school and spoke from my heart.
Hoping the kids would give me a fresh start.

"The spots on my shirts won't change how I live.
Being kind and helpful is my way to give."

"The pictures have shown, upon further inspection;
because of his love, we became his reflection."

"Before we could ask, he opened the door;
he revealed a new world for us to explore."

"Your name was 'A Mouse'; that fact was so clear.
Verified each day by one look in the mirror.
Our hearts grow in goodness. It's where we belong.
It's very clear now, that we've had your name wrong!"

"You came to our school excited to learn.
Some kids were mean, but you'd always return.
You opened our hearts by being so nice,
and taught us to be more friendly to mice."

"You showed us no act of kindness is small.
Each time you were needed, you answered the call."

"The heart on your chest is as BIG as a house.
It's no longer secret. You're Amazing Mouse!"

21

You don't need a tail to share a good feeling,
with one simple smile the hurts begin healing.
When you are nice to others each day,
kindness will flow and Love finds the way.

Our outsides look different, on that I agree.
Look inside your chest and discover the key.
We share the same heart in color and shape.
Be kind to others and you'll find your cape!

"Love's stronger than fear. We all know that's true.
The heart on our chests has made its debut.
The world needs our help. We're on the same team.
We're all Kindness Heroes. We dream the same dream."

23

"Believe hearts can fly and follow the breeze.
A world filled with kindness is better than cheese!"

THE END

The end? I don't think so. The beginning? Not quite!
Amazing Mouse wants to take one more bite.

The world is filled with cheese that is tasty.
Stay tuned for more fun. Ending now would be hasty.

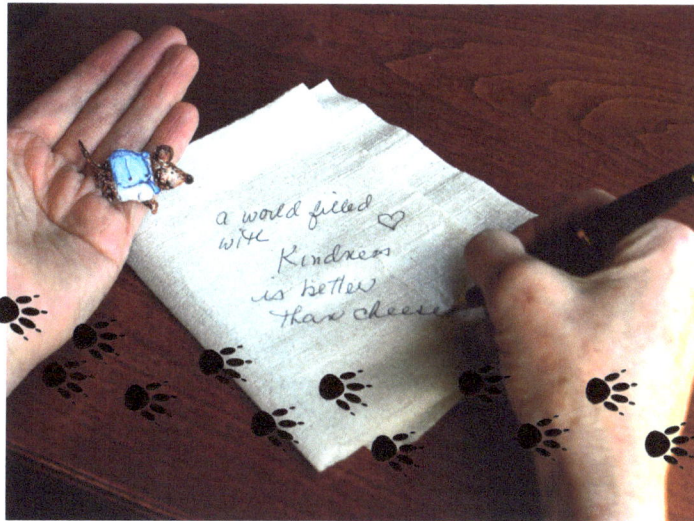

About the Author

Cam A Vuksinich believes "Hearts are for Loving." Her favorite thing about this project was meeting Amazing Mouse for the first time. He most likely lived in her head for most of her life but it wasn't until he made his way into her heart that they met for the first time and a life-long friendship was born.

As Winnie the Pooh says, "Sometimes, the smallest things take up the most room in your heart."

You may contact Cam at camv@AmazingMouseBooks.com

About the Illustrator

L. M. Hargrave believes "Hands are to make things." Her favorite part about this project is the idea that kids so freely love the impossible—whether a mouse at school or infectious goodness in the world. Making these pictures encouraged her to embrace "Amazing" and she hopes they do the same for you!

You may contact Lindy at lindy.hargrave@gmail.com

Amazing Mouse Books

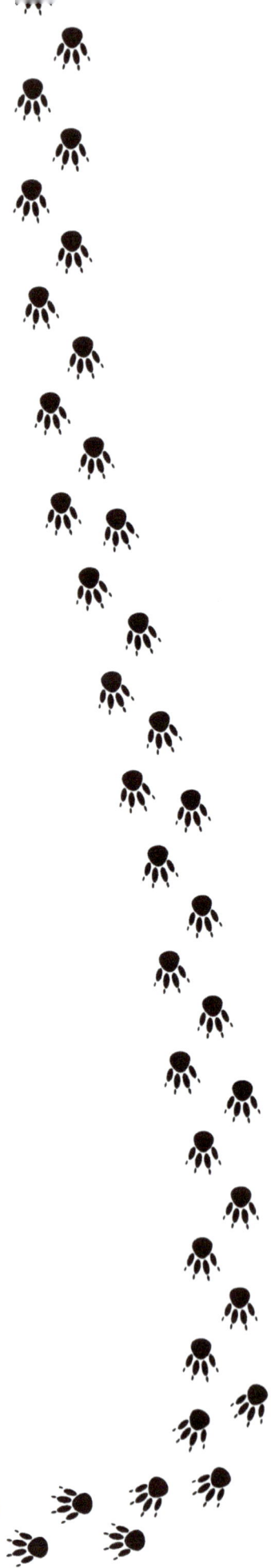

Ready for More Adventures with Amazing Mouse??

♥ Count the number of mice in the title. They're sneaky! Did you find them all?

♥ Find all the hearts in the book? How many did you discover? Where's your heart?

♥ Look closely and see if you can find all the spills in the book?

♥ Can you find our favorite mouse? How many times is AM pictured in the book?

♥ Find the cheese and count the pieces.

♥ This book is dedicated to people who choose to be kind. Are you kind?

♥ Tell a story about kindness.

Page 1

Why is AM being held in the air in the picture?

What color is Daddy Mouse's tie?

What color is Mama Mouse's apron?

What color is AM's backpack?

Page 2

Find the Question Marks. How many do you find? What is he thinking?

Page 3

Count the number of kids. How many do you see?

Look at the boy standing on the chair. What color is his shirt?

Look at the girl sitting in the wheelchair. What color is her hair?

Find AM. Why are they pointing at him?

Page 4

Name the items on the teacher's desk. On the floor?

How did AM get up to the shelf on the chalk board?

What do you see in the thought bubbles?

Page 5

What changed on the teacher's desk? Why?

Find the spill on the teacher's desk.

Page 6-7

What does AM have in his hand? What is he doing?

Find the missing pepperoni.

What flavor is the soda? What's your favorite flavor?

Page 8

What happened to AM's shirt?

What color is the spot on his shirt?

Page 9

Find AM's shirt.

How many thoughts bubbles to you see?

What is AM thinking? Bubble 1? Bubble 2? Bubble 3? Bubble 4?

Page 10

What color is AM's spot?

Why are the spots always red?

Page 11

Why does AM have an umbrella?

Why is he looking at the sunny sky?

Page 12

What is happening to AM's shirts in the machine?

Look at the kids shirts. Why are they upset?

Page 13

How many spots can you see?

What is causing the spots to appear?

Page 14

Look at the school sign. Look at page 2. What's different?

What did AM say on page 1? It started with "S"......?

Page 15

Can you find the hidden spill?

What items do you see on the teacher's desk?

Why is AM on the top of the desk? How did he get there?

Page 16

Uh oh! Another hidden spill. Can you find it?

Why is the teacher looking at the pictures?

Who do you see in each picture on the wall?

Why is AM always in the pictures of kindness?

Page 17

Who is holding the door? Why?

Who is he helping?

Page 18

Look at the reflection in the glass door. What do you see on AM's shirt?

The spot changed its shape. Look closely and guess what happened.

Page 19

What is the teacher explaining to AM about the pictures?

Can you find AM? Who's holding him so can see the pictures?

Page 20

Notice the sign on the building. It starts with "S" and ends with "ool." What is the word?

Look at the teacher. She is taking something out of her pocket. What is it?

Page 21

What do you see on all the kids shirts?

Count the hearts in the picture

How did Amazing Mouse make their hearts appear?

Look at page number 20. It's a spill. Look at page number 21. What do you see?

Page 22

What has changed about Amazing Mouse?

He's touching a plant. Can you name it?

Look at the biggest dandelion. There's a tiny secret hidden in the fluff. Can you find it?

Page 23

Why are the kids looking at the sky?

Find the hidden heart.

Page 24

If you look really close, you'll discover the secret. The lady bug's spot has changed.

Why did her spot change?

What happens when hearts touch hearts?

Do you know hearts can fly? How can you make your heart fly?

Page 25

Look at the picture. Look at the front cover. What is different? What happened?

Whose footprints do you see walking all over the pages at the end?

Follow the prints and you'll discover the answer.........

Who is your new best friend? Clue? He has a tail and he loves YOU!

♥ Guess what? You answered ALL the questions! Yay for YOU! You are AMAZING!!

♥ Download your official Red Cape Club Card at www.amazingmousebooks.com

One more thing....

♥ What is Amazing Mouse's favorite game? Hide and Squeak!

For more fun riddles visit us at www.amazingmousebooks.com.

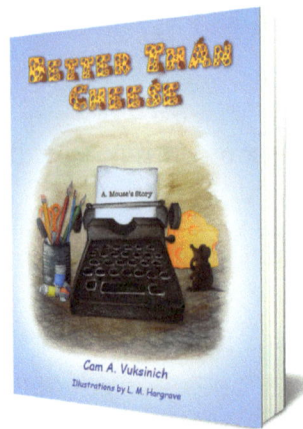

Buy a Book. Give a Book.

You've made Amazing Mouse very happy!! Thank you for buying his book!!

His dream is to give his books to children in schools, hospitals, homeless shelters, as well as, the countless invisible heroes, small and big, who do the right thing every day.

Amazing Mouse applauds your service!!
www.amazingmousebooks.com

All proceeds from the sale of this book will be donated to help Amazing Mouse share his book with those in need and support the mission of the One World Heart Project, a public charity dedicated to inspiring a more compassionate society by educating people about the health benefits of good deeds and empowering them to live more fulfilling lives.

www.oneworldheartproject.org

www.ingramcontent.com/pod-product-compliance
Lightning Source LLC
Chambersburg PA
CBHW042103040426
42448CB00002B/128